Unearthing His Treasures

J. K. Sanchez

All scripture quotations are taken from The ESV Bible (The Holy Bible, English Standard Version).

Unearthing His Treasures
ISBN – 978-0-578-49183-7

Published by: Button Lane Books Spanaway, WA 98387
Contact: jksanchez@gmail.com - www.jksanchez.com

Cover Photography and all internal photos by:
J.K.Sanchez Photography
Original paintings by: D.L.Sanchez

Cover Design by:
Button Lane Books www.jksanchez.com

Dedication

To my children, Amber, David & Daniel and your love of treasure hunting that always inspires me. My greatest desire is that you find the hidden treasures He has for your life.

To those who desire to live a life in search of the treasures of Heaven. He is faithful to open your eyes to the hidden, life-changing jewels that surround you.

To my God and Savior Jesus Christ – UNTO YOU BE ALL THE GLORY!

Contents

Acknowledgments

First and foremost, I am thankful for the support and consistent overflow of love from my husband, Dennis, my children, their spouses and my grandchildren. My overwhelming JOY is found in each of your faces.

A huge thanks to Amber Lynn Sanchez for all your hours of passionate commitment to editing every letter, phrase and comma – and so much more!

Thank you, my friend, Tamara Maus for always encouraging and for sharing your detail ability in proofing.

And finally – but above all – my thanks to Jesus Christ who directs, inspires, and teaches me daily to walk in His rest. There I live a life in search of His hidden treasures.

My life is not my own but a gift freely given back to the one who gave His life for me.

Introduction

Treasures are found all around us, but taking time to stop, see and consider them takes practice. Unearthing those treasures requires reflection, a forgotten discipline in this "plugged-in" society.

Unearthing His Treasures *will help you dig deeper into everyday-life comparisons, finding spiritually-motivating similarities. As you find these hidden treasures you will be drawn to the feet of Jesus. Begin your day with a time of reflection as His treasures, become yours.*

Our search for treasure begins at birth, while gasping for our first breath. As we grow and learn, we fine-tune our search engine to include every aspect of life, from beginning to end.

There are many forms of treasure that can be searched for: those hidden deep in the earth, those laying out on top of the surface, those resting on the ocean floor, and those within books and lives.

My love of treasure hunting must have been ignited as my sisters and I played in the dirt, making mud pies and hoping to dig all the way to China. And now that same love has been passed on to my children!

We'd hunt for hours on beaches, looking for the best shell or "the one" special rock that had to come home with us. All of these ended up in memory-filled piles, and now lay embedded in concrete on our back-yard path – permanent reminders of those wonderful hunts.

Who hunts for treasures? We all do, in one way or another. Almost all professions are in search of something – looking for treasure in hidden places; accountants, lawyers, doctors, electricians, archeologists, ecologists, pastors… and the list goes on and on.

Spiritually, we are treasure hunting every day of our lives. How we view our environment, relationships and daily tasks is all part of finding treasure; it is the beginning of the one-true hunt. I have found this hunt when I willingly exchanged my life for the one that Christ purchased for me. It lasts throughout a lifetime, driven forward as I search for the purpose I was created to express.

Matthew 13:45 *Again, the kingdom of heaven is like a merchant in search of fine pearls, who, on finding one pearl of great value, went and sold all that he had and bought it.*

My desire is finding treasure of eternal value, life-changing in both the spiritual and the natural – they are found in hidden places. I often find them in the bible and during intimate times with Jesus, as well as, in everyday life and in the lives of those who surround me.

A treasure that continually amazes me is found when I open my bible and read. In the same passages that I've read over and over, I find new revelations that I have never seen.

The bible is truly new every morning – we see it through new lenses of life, daily. As we listen and are led, new directions and revelations are opened up to us and change us.

So, my treasure hunt begins afresh every morning as I unearth His treasures.

His treasures fill each of us! Let's dig and make mud pies, and see how He directs us to find the best shells and perfect rocks that He has planned to use to adorn His kingdom – using you.

We Are Never Empty

As she wrestled with sleep through the late hours into the morning, she dreamt. She awoke over and over from a similar dream – quickly falling back to sleep, just to dream another version. This puzzling dream was filled with only one thing – open boxes. All the boxes were different in size, construction and material, but all were empty. As the questions swirled in her head, she began to question God and wait for an answer, "What does this mean? What do I do with it?"

Later that morning, she soon found herself listening to her pastor explain a tradition of the Feast of Tabernacles – which included the drawing of water and empty cisterns. In Latin, *cisterns* translate to *boxes*. Her galloping heart stirred as she sat transfixed, waiting for God's revelation.

Days later, as understanding marinated in her spirit, the Holy Spirit's direction brought expectation to her heart.

We, the bride of Christ, have allowed our cisterns (the place of His indwelling presence), to grow cold and empty – thus, many empty boxes.

How easily we trudge through life in the midst of chaos, pain and distraction; never realizing that each hit we take from those we love, physical ailments, financial struggles and living in a crazy "on-the-edge" world, all sucks the water from our own cisterns. We live in a state of constant empty boxes – our cisterns have been depleted – and that is the insidious lie! We have been given full cisterns – ALL the time – it's a sustainable promise! The Spirit dwells within us; we are never empty – we just don't take time to dip in and drink.

Within each of us resides the Spirit of God through Christ – we have all we need within us. Jesus has given us a river of living water that is available to us ALL the time. We don't have to live a life with dry, empty cisterns. Just stop, dip in and you will find water available! Begin to walk in a life filled with thanksgiving and praise! Yes, in the very midst of all that sucks you dry, there you will soon find that your cistern is no longer dry, but has begun to flow. Joy will bring relief – and though life may still be in the same state, you will find the journey now flows differently within your heart.

John 4:10 Jesus answered her, "if you knew the gift of God, and who it is that is saying to you, 'Give me a drink,' you would have asked him, and he would have given you living water."

John 4: 14 but whoever drinks of the water that I will give him will never be thirsty again. The water that I will give him will become in him a spring of water welling up to eternal life."

Personal Insights:

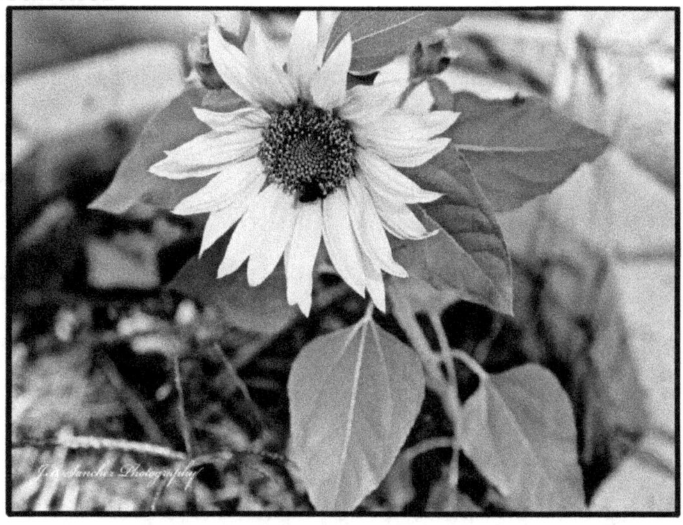

Beauty in the Firepit

As the warm, summer sun continued to march forward toward fall, its rays allowed sunflowers to flourish in the yard. These same summer rays also limited the ability to burn in the firepit – it sat unused, filled with scraps of yard debris, wood and weeds.

With great surprise, the firepit now boasted of a single beauty – yep, a sunflower. Right there in the midst of all the debris, right there, where no water had been provided, right there, where only rock supported its roots: there erupted a single beauty – her head held high – a single sunflower.

Contemplation of this flower's unusual bedding choice, provides a spiritual abstract. Beauty can come out of the midst of chaos, out of the midst of barren dryness, or out of the difficult places you live in. From the depths of your pain and loss, beauty can emerge.

How does that happen in our lives? It comes from the exceptional quality of seed that the cross of Jesus provides us and a choice of our heart. Willingness to allow the Spirit of God to heal, strengthen, and mature the seed of faith that's been dropped into our mess, is a decision. If we look to Him – right there in the midst of the chaos, right there, where all is barren and dry, right there, where all is hard and difficult – suddenly, there will erupt a single beauty, her head held high. A victorious example of who He has created you to be will proudly stand in the middle of your firepit.

Your God is faithful to bring beauty out of the most unexpected difficult situations in your life. He has lovingly offered you the seed of His Son and it's been placed within your heart – you only need to choose to receive it, believe it, and wait.

Trust Him to complete the work. His timing is perfect and His timing produces the beauty hidden in that dark, barren place.

Philippians 1:6 And I am sure of this, that he who began a good work in you will bring it to completion at the day of Jesus Christ.

Personal Insights:

"You'd Better Soak That"

Today, words that I have spoken probably a hundred times in my lifetime – *"You'd better soak that,"* jumped out at me as a source of pondering.

Soaking something means that it becomes saturated for a purpose. We soak a grime-covered pan, a stained piece of cloth, and even a dried-up pot of soil. The purpose is to change it, to remove the grime, the stain or, in the case of soil, to till it, and prepare it for something new to take root.

In the Christian church culture, the word "soak" (meaning to wait in a posture of silent pray, for extended periods of time) has run its course of the "in thing." But in reality, it is there, in that silent posture that we are changed. As we wait at the feet of Jesus, as we are still in his presence, as we listen in our prayer closets – we are "soaking" in the very present environment of a life-giving, life-changing, life-speaking Holy Spirit that loves to talk. It is in this place that we receive the peace that surpasses all understanding.

Our busy lives make it difficult to slow down and take that time to be still – but if we don't, we live in a constant spin of chaos. Peace comes from that quiet place of trusting our Jesus. It is during these times that we allow our grime and stains to be removed, and our dried-up soil to be saturated and tilled. And then we are ready to receive something new that will take root and bloom in our lives.

Take time to "soak" – sit, be still, listen and receive – and you will be amazed how His presence will refresh you, give you strength for the day ahead, and transform all areas of your life.

Psalm 46:10a " Be still, and know that I am God."

Philippians. 4:7 And the peace of God, which surpasses all understanding, will guard your hearts and your minds in Christ Jesus.

Personal Insights:

Speak Life

Life is full of, "the good, the bad and the ugly." But today, let's focus on the fact that the first in that well-known quote is "the GOOD." Life *IS* full of good – it is all around us, if we look.

Unfortunately, we are inundated with the negative. We hear it and see it everywhere. The news visually captivates the worst-of-the-worst, it pours in through our televisions, the radio screams it in our ears, and it jumps off the page as we scroll through an endless social media feed.

Somewhere within our senses, we've become calloused and obsessed with the bad – forgetting that there is good. That callousness easily fuels and changes our hearts. Soon, we have become bitter and continually negative – everything is tainted by that bend in our thinking.

To change a negative behavior, we must make a choice. A concerted effort to turn off that "bad and ugly" input, and to look around and find "the GOOD."

Join me today in an effort that will renew your life – an effort to find the "GOOD" in every atmosphere you engage in. Begin by speaking life to those around you and watch the transformation happen.

Philippians 4:8 Finally, brothers, whatever is true, whatever is honorable, whatever is just, whatever is pure, whatever is lovely, whatever is commendable, if there is any excellence, if there is anything worthy of praise, think about these things.

Personal Insights:

____

____

____

____

____

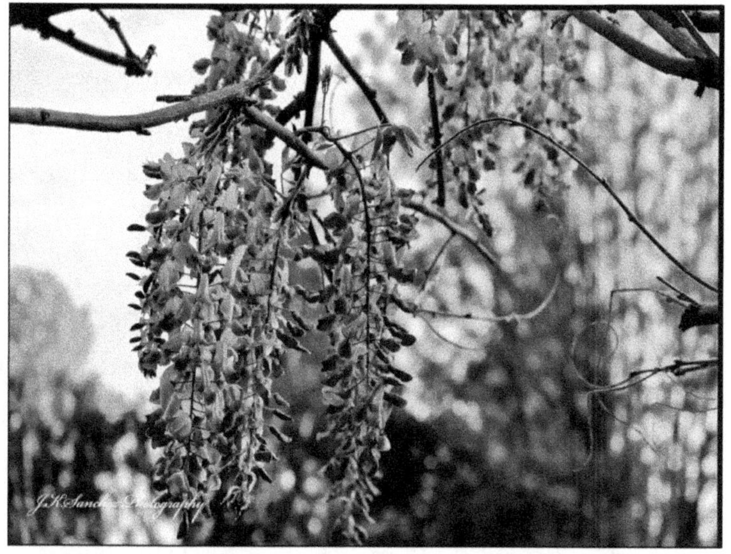

Stronger & Higher Together

With a six-foot wooden fence between them, my twenty-foot majestic 'Purple Robe' tree stands beside my neighbor's spectacular wisteria vine – both prolific in growth and multiplication. Shoots abound underground – both ways – between the fence line. Each spring through early summer, both flower with intoxicating floral blooms that are glorious to behold. This summer, however, I have noticed an exciting merging of the two.

The wisteria, now strong and flourishing, has "jumped the fence" and has begun intertwining with the strength and height of the 'Purple Robe', reaching its tendrils higher than it previously could. OH MY – anticipation waits for next spring's glorious sight as they erupt – stronger together and each increasing the other's beauty – transforming from glory to glory.

Spiritually, we are also meant to periodically "jump the fence". Those who believe in Christ are many – many different individuals in many different buildings – each prolific and multiplying in their own sphere. As one body through Christ, it's OK to "jump the fence": to intertwine and to bring the beauty of one into many.

Individually, we plant our roots into a single place of growth (our church); there we are safe, nurtured, grow, and produce. Upon reaching the top of that six-foot fence, our strength then can be shared, expanded and enlarged into the body of Christ around us.

We as a body require and thrive in unity and connection of each member, whether that is individually or as complete groups of believers. We are all one in Christ!

Just as the strength of the 'Purple Robe' will support the continued expansion of the wisteria vine (even over the fence), so should we strengthen and support our sisters and brothers in faith.

Together we will produce the glorious sight of growing from Glory to Glory. We will grow stronger and higher as we become one body – loving and walking together.

<u>I Corinthians 12: 12-13</u> For just as the body is one and has many members, and all the members of the body, though many, are one body, so it is with Christ. For in one Spirit we were all baptized into one body – Jews or Greeks, slaves or free – and all were made to drink of one Spirit.

<u>Personal Insights:</u>

Faith Like Honey

I recently pulled out a bottle of honey and noticed it had begun to crystallize. I dipped my spoon in anyway and it quickly adhered. However, it was so thick that the spoon wouldn't lift out! But as I placed the jar in a pan of warm water, it soon softened back to its normal, yummy consistency.

As this little morning event transpired, I was drawn to a spiritual parallel: faith is like honey! It is a substance that is thick, draws things to it, and changes anything it touches. It only requires a small amount to achieve its effect, and it is addictive in its flavor.

Faith requires only one thing: that we believe. With honey, we must believe it is sweet before we reach out to taste it – so it is with faith. Once we believe, faith is ignited and begins its transforming affect.

As we have looked at honey's qualities, so should our faith qualities parallel. Our faith in Christ should be deep and thick – a relationship that has substance and that transforms who we are and everything we touch. Our faith should be contagious and draw others to us – sincere and full of love, and not pushy or overly-sweet in its presentation, but full of love. Our faith should be addictive – both to us and to those around us.

This transforming effect isn't something we can *work at,* but just IS as we walk by faith and not by our sight. Our love of Christ and desire for His presence will ignite our mustard-seed faith, then it will produce a tree of faith that will draw into our lives all that the Kingdom of Heaven has for us – just like the honey sucked in my spoon.

How is your faith consistency?
Is it rich and thick?
Is it crystallizing?

If it is rich and thick, then keep it flowing and watch the transformation around you. As you dig deeper into His presence, it will keep flowing, and draw others – and its addictively-sweet flavor will fuel your desire and love for His presence more and more.

However, we sometimes carry our faith through years of life without using it. Then, like the honey, it becomes crystallized – thick and unusable. But, just like my honey, it only takes a little warming to adjust its consistency. Our faith can be rewarmed by simply stepping back to the place our faith began: at the feet of Jesus.

II Corinthians. 5:7 *for we walk by faith, not by sight.*

I John 5:4-5. *For everyone who has been born of God overcomes the world. And this is the victory that has overcome the world - our faith. Who is it that overcomes the world except the one who believes that Jesus is the Son of God?*

Personal Insights:

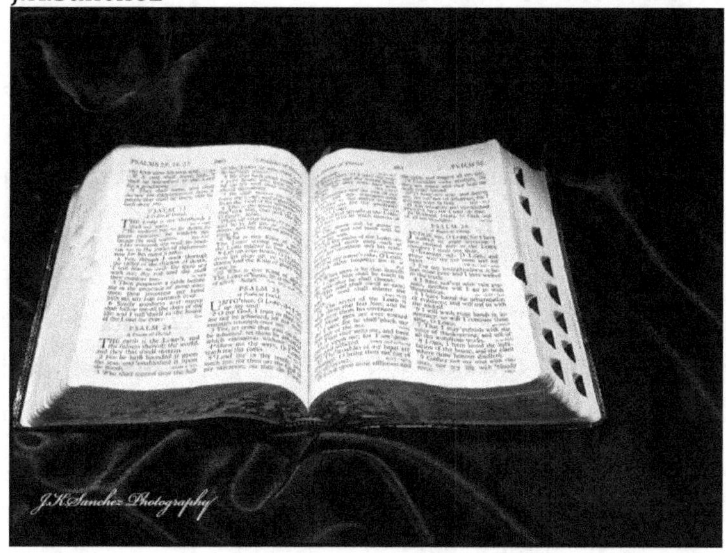

On the Road

In disappointment, confusion and hopelessness, the miles to travel toward Emmaus left room for the disciples to vent to one another. And then – along came a stranger that drew near and joined their walk. Not knowing who this stranger was, the story of the origin of their sadness was poured out as they stopped in their tracks on this dusty road. After much time together that day, they recognized him only as they sat to eat and he broke the bread – but then he was gone.

They said to each other, "Did not our hearts burn within us while he talked to us on the road, while he opened to us the Scriptures?" *(Luke 24:32)*

We, too – when clouded by disappointment, confusion and hopelessness – often don't look up, don't hear and don't see our Savior right there on the dusty road with us.

He still comes alongside – drawing near – as we walk this difficult journey. He still opens to us the scriptures. He still speaks words of comfort and encouragement. Those words that will burn within our hearts; are found in a living book! There is only one book that can do that – and it is alive and new every morning! This living book is the Word of God – letters on a page that will open up to us the Kingdom of God.

How can that be?

No matter how many days, years or decades you have read this book – *today* it can burn within your heart a new understanding, a new revelation. As you lift this book, read, and allow the spirit of God to speak, it changes from words on a page, to understanding, to revelation, and finally, transformation on your dusty road is eminent.

As you walk this road of life, pick up His Word! Allow His words to be opened to you, to burn within your heart, to lift the heaviness that life has thrown at you; it is here that you will find life – a life abundant.

Hebrews 4:12 For the word of God is living and active, sharper than any two-edged sword, piercing to the division of soul and of spirit, of joints and of marrow, and discerning the thoughts and intentions of the heart.

Personal Insights:

One Missing Piece

I love puzzles, and several times a year (usually during winter or a nasty cold bug) I binge on them. Inevitably, this process ends in "one missing piece." With two little dachshunds at my feet and their love of eating cardboard paper, getting to the completion of a puzzle without having lost a piece is almost unheard of. Though, I still love the process and have learned to enjoy the picture that has presented itself, there is just something disheartening when I see that one gaping hole.

As I look at my recent creation with its one missing piece, I am struck by the thought that our lives are often like this puzzle. Pieces are fit together and begin to create a beautiful picture that represents our journey in this life.

Each section of the puzzle shows life's endeavors: our relationships, our jobs, our adventures. But there's one missing piece – the piece needed to hold the whole picture together. It will never be complete with that empty space that begins to loom. You can look at the picture's overall beauty, but that gaping hole is obvious. WE can't fix it, but it can be fixed, and Jesus gave us the solution.

Jesus came to make you whole – to bind up the places that are frayed, broken and missing. He gave you the missing piece, free of charge. The piece that completes your life, the one that makes you whole and brings all those other pieces together into one beautiful picture. That picture is one of a life to be lived in abundance, that is given to you from the hand of a loving heavenly Father. You just need to reach out and pick up that offered piece from the nail-scarred hand of Jesus.

If you find your puzzle missing that one piece, simply say "YES" and pick it up.

John 3:16 For God so loved the world, that he gave his only Son, that whoever believes in him should not perish but have eternal life.

John 10:10-11 The thief comes only to steal and kill and destroy. I came that they may have life and have it abundantly. I am the good shepherd. The good shepherd lays down his life for the sheep.

Personal Insights:

____

____

____

____

____

____

____

____

<u>Keep Out the Weeds</u>

Weeds, weeds, weeds! If I desired to grow only weeds, I would have a garden paradise with no effort. I could <u>choose</u> to let those weeds go, flourishing in their own right, for many are pretty as they bloom. But I love flowers, so a continual effort of picking, pulling, and digging is required – spring through fall. Keeping my flowerbeds happy and productive often proves to be back-and-knee-breaking work.

The effort has its own reward though, as my plants and flowers are freed from the weeds that steal their nutrients and space, they begin to flourish and grow into what they were created to be.

Awe… just like us! Weeds crop up, often unbeknownst to us. We can indulge them and allow them to grow; saying to ourselves *it's easier, maybe no one will notice, or it is our choice, right?* Or, we can grab the garden implements and get them out.

Your choices each day can allow the seeds of many types of weeds to be distributed all around you. Suddenly, you will find those weeds choking out your life's nutrients and crowding out what is important. Many of those choices seem good – they don't look bad, or won't hurt you – but deep down in the roots they are determining if and how you will grow into all you were created to be.

Pulling, picking and digging those weeds out of your life will take effort – back-and-knee-breaking effort. In fact, keeping out the weeds requires a daily diligence of looking to and listening to the Holy Spirit as He enlightens exactly where the weeds need to be attended to.

Thankfully, cleaning out the weeds of wrong choices is well worth the effort and rather simple. Begin making all your life choices as you abide in His love – choices that speak loudly of your desire to serve Christ, and not your own desires. These types of choices will allow the weeding process to become easier. The reward will become apparent as your life begins to flourish and grow – showing forth the beauty of whom you were created to be.

Choose today to keep those weeds out, and you will flourish as His Kingdom garden.

John 15:8-9 By this my Father is glorified, that you bear much fruit and so prove to be my disciples. As the Father has loved me, so have I loved you. Abide in my love.

Personal Insights:

Walking Between Belief and Faith

When spring arrives, *momma* bird is preparing for new life that will begin within her nest. Soon, it will hold tiny lives readying for release. Each step for their little lives, will require a physical adjustment.

The new babies find strength within to begin the pecking process to come into the world – If they never worked at pecking that shell open, they would die.

Once they break free from the protective shell, they must be fed from *momma.* They can believe and expect food, but unless they have the faith to open their little beaks to receive it, they will die.

As they grow stronger, and fuzz becomes feathers, they must then take another big step of faith. They have seen *momma* fly in and out of the nest, but just peaking over the edge is a scary thing. They get encouraged and nudged by *momma*, but believing still isn't enough; they must have the faith to step over the edge, free fall, and lift off. If they choose to stay in the nest, they will eventually die.

Once the flight ability occurs, they still have much to learn. Each step in the growth process requires belief in what is being taught to them, as well as faith to step out and do it. But once they do – oh, what a beautiful world they have to enjoy! They fly higher and sing boldly of the greatness of creation.

The whole process takes a short time, but is one of walking between belief and faith.

Spiritually, we also live a life walking between belief and faith. We can walk a life full of believing in who God is, what the Bible says and what Jesus did for us. But, somewhere faith must begin to churn inside; in this place, belief changes and faith emerges. This faith begins pushing us to move into a place where we take the step over the edge, free fall, and lift off.

It is here, at lift off, that the transformation of the blood of Christ changes us to BE HIS representative on the earth. As we listen to the Holy Spirit and are directed and encouraged, it then takes a tiny bit of faith to say, "YES LORD." Then we take full flight in all HE has created us to be, and begin to fly higher and sing boldly of the greatness of our Lord.

Let's join our feathered friends: step out, free fall, and lift off to higher places.

II Corinthians. 5:7 for we walk by faith, not sight

I Thessalonians. 5:24 He who calls you is faithful; he will surely do it.

Personal Insights:

Short-term Life in a Bud Vase

I love flowers – pretty much ALL of them – but my favorites are those with a lingering, intoxicating scent. In the Pacific Northwest, roses are rather temperamental due to our abundance of rain, and most of mine end up bedraggled. However, this year I decided to find the perfect one; I potted it and planned to carefully tend it. The first two buds appeared, and expectantly I watched as they began their slow burst into bloom. OH, what reward!

They uncurled with glorious swirls of yellows, oranges and crimson, along with a smell that was heavenly. They were allowed several days on the stems before a torrential downpour came. As the rain began pelting down, I darted out to protect them from destruction – the only way, was to cut them off and bring them inside. The scent that filled my living area was quickly released as they accepted a short-term life in a bud vase. They quickly opened, continuing to show off their splendor of colors, while their scent seemed to grow stronger.

Each day when I was writing I sat in front of my beauties and was blessed to breathe in a scent that made me smile – one that continued to grow as the petals faded. Eventually, the petals began to drop to the table, but the scent was still my writing companion. Soon, they found a few more days as they resided in a small crystal dish by my laptop – their scent lingering as a little reminder that they weren't gone.

We, like my roses, live a short-term life in a bud vase. We show forth our colors (our gifts and talents) throughout that time, but do we leave a continual aroma? Is ours one of sweet enjoyment or do we carry an uninviting one? What is our life-changing fragrance that lingers and intoxicates?

With Christ as your eternal life source, you become that sweet, intoxicating aroma that draws life and invites others to partake.

Without the presence of Christ as your focus, your flower is beautiful but the scent – like my daisies' – is not one that others desire.

Your time is fleeting, limited and fading, but when you walk this life journey spreading the fragrance of Christ, you will be as my fading roses – a scent that will linger as a reminder that through Christ you are present – now and forever.

As you continue your life with Christ, allow your fragrance to become a sweet, intoxicating aroma as you walk out your journey of short-term life in a bud vase.

II Corinthians 2:14 But thanks be to God, who in Christ always leads us in triumphal procession, and through us spreads the fragrance of the knowledge of him everywhere.

Personal Insights:

Grandma Blankets

While pregnant with my daughter, I began a craft – one that has covered babies for over forty years. Now, hundreds, upon hundreds, of blankets have been made to warm many little bodies – each blanket made from yarn or fabric and each covered with love and prayer.

Recently, I began to hear and see what I never expected – as these children are now much older and even becoming adults, they still have their "grandma blankets." Now, tattered, torn, and covered with patches, they still cherish those "blankies."

Why?
It's just a piece of fabric, long outgrown.

Second-hand stores are filled with old, beat-up blankets.
But these seem to be different, held in unusually-high regard.

As I pondered this, I felt the Spirit of the Lord speak. He reminded me that every blanket I have made specifically for that special little one (or now special loved one) was soaked in prayer as each stitch was added.

When they cuddle down into the blanket's warmth, it's that love that is felt as it saturates and covers them. It brings peace and comfort, so that years later – when hard, painful times are faced – the heart, the mind, and the emotions return to think of the "blankie" and the comfort found there. So, they keep it – treasure it – and fold it away for another time to be reminded of the comfort found there.

Those "blankies" are simply an earthly example of a heavenly, eternal comfort that is available to us all. So, for now, I have been blessed to pass on a little bit of heaven's love to the "littles" (and "not-so-littles") around me with those "grandma blankets."

Each act of love that we pour out will reap a harvest! Whatever your hands find to do, do it in love and it will impact those around you. The outcome may not be seen here, but it is bringing a touch of love and heaven into another's life. That touch may be just what they need to find comfort and to give them hope.

II Corinthians 1:3-4 Blessed be the God and Father of our
Lord Jesus Christ, the Father of mercies and
God of all comfort,
who comforts us in all our affliction,
so that we may be able to comfort
those who are in any affliction,
with the comfort with which we ourselves are
comforted by God.

Personal Insights:

A Place of Pause

Some mornings are made for sleeping in. Some are made to jump up and get going, for they are pre-planned and full of expectation. Then, there are mornings where you get that early-morning wake-up call in your spirit. When those mornings occur, we expect a direction to pray, study – *or do something.* But when it becomes quiet, we question why we are awake early with no apparent purpose. These are the days we should relish – for our Lord has called us to His feet to wait.

As we learn to hear and move only as the Spirit leads, there often comes a place of pause. This place requires discipline and peace to wait and rest in the midst of great anticipation. This place of pause is much harder than being called to make a move, because our tendency is to take it into our own hands and just get it done. But that's not how it works in the Kingdom of Heaven.

To run ahead or lag behind is loss, but to wait and only move in synchronized, perfect timing with the Spirit's call is of great gain. However, it comes with a great cost. That cost is to wait! Waiting is much harder than it sounds as we prayerfully prepare for His call to move.

Perfect timing, moving on-time and waiting is found throughout the Bible. The children of Israel only moved when the cloud-by-day or pillar-by-night moved. The ten virgins had lamps full of oil and waited for the bridegroom. Jesus went where and when the Father directed, bringing life exactly where the Father was moving. The apostles, directed by the Spirit, carried the gospel to all parts of the world. But, what does that look like to us? Exactly the same: simply wait, wait and wait until we hear His voice to move. Then as we are walking in peace and rest, totally at a readiness of spirit, anxiety free; we can then move as He directs.

So, my message to you is one of waiting, listening and being ready for the call and direction of the bridegroom – with lamps filled with oil, you are to wait in His presence for His stirring and movement. In this time of pause, your heart will be made ready to receive and to quickly move. Your heart then will erupt with a joyous shout of, "YES, LORD!"

Psalm 27:14 Wait for the Lord; be strong and
let your heart take
courage; wait for the Lord!

Personal Insights:

____

____

____

____

____

____

____

Who's in Your Boat?

The darkening clouds began to swiftly swirl around them as the waves surged. The sea having been tame as the short journey began, now churned with waves crashing over the bow and threatening to take their lives. They had seen His hands do many miracles – how and why was He sleeping as they struggled in the midst of this aggressive storm? Waking Him from his slumber brought rebuke – first for their lack of faith, but then of the very wind and waves that threatened their lives. Quickly, the tumultuous sea became still as they stood astonished at His authority.

As we walk through life's journey we are also surprised by storms that threaten our lives – some mild, some crashing the bow, and some that have begun to sink our boats. How we respond and how we get through it, depends on WHO is in our boat.

All of us begin to falter, question and grow weary in the midst of the storm. However, if you know Jesus is your rock, your salvation and your hope, then you know He is in your boat. He is always there for you and has your back! Going down with the boat is NOT His plan! You simply need to wake up – look up – and with faith, reach out for His hand.

It's not in your ability to silence the storm. You only need to look to Him and He steps in. He rebukes the winds and waves; He calms the storm.

Matthew 8:26 And he said to them, "Why are you afraid, O you of little faith?" Then he rose and rebuked the winds and the sea, and there was a great calm.

Personal Insights:

Out-of-the-Box Proposal

An excited young man began logistically planning a life-time event: he set up a marriage proposal and his girlfriend unsuspectingly would be a participant. A front-row seat was acquired at a well-known magician's show. The plan quickly materialized as the magician stepped down to take her hand to be his assistant for a particular illusion. A huge box was seen to be empty as she checked inside and all around it – then it was closed up tight and turned completely around. The box was then re-opened and – to her utter amazement – out stepped her boy-friend. Ring box in hand, he took the one-knee pose and presented to her his request to be his wife. Her expectations of this night where totally blown out of the water. That box held a new life – a new abundance that was not expected.

Our expectations of life, of dreams, and even of God, are mostly prepackaged and boxed into our personal paradigm of tidy thinking. But I have found that the older we get, the less "boxed" those expectations seem to be.

Over the years, most of those boxes have come up empty. By trusting God with all that was previously stuffed in them I have chosen to do the best thing: take the empty boxes and close them up, or – even better – get rid of them all together.

The funny thing is, our God never seems to work within our exceptions or on our timetables. His plans and purposes for our lives can never fit in our small thinking or our prepacked boxes.

Jesus likes to surprise us – to step out of the box and present us with new life options, outrageous abundance, and all things unexpected. His box is so much better than what we could ever expect.

When we step out, say YES and accept His request for participation – *watch out* – we have just been given access to more than we can think or imagine. That's just how good HE is!

Join me on stage to accept His proposal and allow your boxes to be blown away.

Ephesians 3:20 Now to him who is able to do far more abundantly than all that we ask or think, according to the power at work within us,

Personal Insights:

Your Spring Will Come

Walking past barren, deciduous trees in early spring, the reminder of the harsh winter is visible all around. However, an interesting event occurs as day after day you make the same passing: one day they are barren – then suddenly, the next day they have burst forth in color. Hidden for those fleeting months, life was sleeping deep inside; it was producing energy to bring forth buds, and conserving power to erupt with new life.

We, too, live through times that are harsh, barren and cold. Life circumstances seem to swirl around us and strip us from all hope, joy and motivation;

emptying our lives and leaving us standing just like those barren deciduous trees.

When your life is dry, barren and broken, you must look forward – toward spring. Your spring waits for the warm touch of your Lord. He knows what is hidden inside of you; what is ready to flourish and what is ready to show forth His glory. His timing and your humility will change your mourning into dancing, and will produce what He has ordained from the beginning of time. Your part is to trust in the spring that is coming, rejoice in the hidden buds being created and at the right time, move in faith into a new and flourishing display of His glory.

Psalm 30:11-12 You have turned for me my mourning into dancing; you have loosed my sackcloth and clothed me with gladness that my glory may sing your praise and not be silent. O Lord my God, I will give thanks to you forever!

Personal Insights:

A Muddy Mess

Fall brings a lot of rain to the Pacific Northwest, and along with it comes mud! My longhaired dachshund loves to help in the yard, and if my hands come in contact with dirt, he believes I have given him automatic free-rein to dive-in, too. His two-inch legs quickly dig a hole that engulfs him head to tail. His passion and love for digging, combined with our soggy seasons, ultimately brings about a soggy, muddy – yet ecstatic – wiggling mess.

So, what does that have to do with the spiritual?

We are rather the same. Our passions and desires can quickly find us covered in mud. Even those passions and desires that are good, profitable and enjoyable can land us in a mud pit. If we allow those passions to run ahead of God's plan for our lives, we can quickly feel overwhelmed, frustrated and... well, rather muddy. We have become distracted from what He desires for our life.

If your passions and desires run you into that place where peace has disappeared then stop – step back – and refocus at the feet of Jesus. Don't keep digging in the mud.

Just as a warm, soapy bath awaits my little muddy buddy, sometimes we, too, need a quick cleansing. And that. is easily found when you look back to the cross of Christ, and wait in His presence. Suddenly, all the mud is washed away and peace reigns. When you trust His leading, and not your own, you will enjoy the bubbles and abide in a promised place of rest.

Psalm 51:10 Create in me a clean heart, O God, and renew a right spirit within me.

Hebrews 10:19-22 Therefore, brothers, since we have confidence to enter the holy places by the blood of Jesus, by the new and living way that he opened for us through the curtain, that is, through his flesh, and since we have a great priest over the house of God, let us draw near with a true heart in full assurance of faith, with our hearts sprinkled clean from an evil conscience and our bodies washed with pure water.

Personal Insights:

____

____

____

____

____

____

____

____

____

Fight Forward

When we are weak and weary, where do we find that strength to stand up again?

What does it mean to be strong?
To be strengthened?

Somewhere deep inside of us is a HERO. The one with the *I-can-do-it* spirit, *chomping at the bit* to keep moving forward – ready take the frontline of battle. This warrior is destined to win. The war cry of "Fight Forward" stirs deep inside, desiring to erupt.

Just when we think we have reached the lowest place, the most helpless and unusable, we reach down inside of our spirit and pull out that one tiny bit of hope. We determine to take the hill one more time – to rescue the "other one" that lays prone before the enemy's attack. That hope and strength doesn't come from us; it is from the Spirit of God.

The story *Brave Heart* is a great one to ruminate over. His purpose wasn't about him – not his desires nor his needs – it was for a greater (much greater) cause.

Being on the frontline of life requires us to take hits now and then, they come at us in physical, emotional and spiritual ways. Some are minimal, and then we keep moving forward; some require us to be carried for recovery to the rear. Then there are those that are near-fatal and require major, home-bound recovery and rehabilitation, as well as a re-purposing of what and where we thought we were going. During each of these we must reach inside, dig deep, and pull from our faith and trust in Christ. Here we find strength. It is at this place we are able to be strong enough to stand up again and overcome.

We often whine and complain about our weaknesses, inabilities and needs – when all God is asking from us is to look outside of ourselves and see what He is calling us to. His desire is for us to be the Hero for someone else and to bring glory to His name. When we choose to see Him only – to respond, rise and fight forward for others – then all our stuff will fall away. When we dig deep inside, we will find the ability to stand up, take the next hill, and rescue the broken before us. It's at that time that we will walk in faith toward abundant life and all the fullness that He has for us. Will our lives miraculously be healed or made whole? Possibly not – but it's in this place we will find strength. We will be strong – not in our own strength, but in His.

Every human spirit has a place where they can reach inside to "keep moving forward;" however, just like the Energizer Bunny, there are times that batteries must be changed. We can accept that and wait on the Lord and those He places in our lives for that purpose – or we can wallow in this rough spot and lose hope.

My choice – my cry – is one of faith in a God who is good to me ALL the time. And I shout, "Fight Forward!"

Isaiah 40:31 but they who wait for the Lord shall renew their strength; they shall mount up with wings like eagles; they shall run and not be weary; they shall walk and not faint.

2Corinthians 12:10 For the sake of Christ, then, I am content with weaknesses,
insults, hardships, persecutions, and calamities.
For when I am weak, then I am strong.

Personal Insights:

His Perfect Wave

The warmth of the sun and the sand, along with the rhythmic movement of the ocean's waves – just feet away – will easily lull the senses into a peace and calm not found many places. But as you lift your eyes and look out to the ocean, you perceive a different story – one of tension and expansive movement.

Previously unnoticed, a lone surfer has passed that calm, warm, sandy beach and persistently slogged through the shallow waves, reaching deeper and deeper. Soon, the only way to go further was to climb onto his surfboard and push against the pressures of the current. He continued his arduous, outward endeavor, going further and further from shore. Seeming to either find the right place or just tiring out, he settles on the board – now sitting and surveying his newly-acquired territory.

We expect him to stand and take each incoming wave. But that is not his plan, to our wonder he allows them, one by one, to pass by as he waits. What is he waiting for? What does he see that we do not? How will he know the right one? When will he move forward?

These questions may never get answered because, as if on cue, he slowly stands as a single, not-so-big swell begins to form. He slowly lifts as the wave takes on a life of its own – growing in height and power. The sound of its approach is exhilarating. The wave's upward movement, the slide forward, and the beautiful delivery down to the warm, waiting sand is exquisite. The surfer, like a dancer on a ballroom floor, sways with each move and sound that this incredible wave produces. This was the wave worth waiting for, and this patient surfer reaped the joy found within – riding this wave upward, forward and through the completion – as he, too, is delivered right out onto the waiting sand. What a spectacular ride!

This picture of an experienced surfer is played out much differently for new surfers. They make many unsuccessful attempts to catch the perfect wave – getting dumped before they reach the top, being pulled under, and even eating and drinking both sand and salt water in the process. Learning the part that patience plays in this sport is what makes it worth the ride.

As we walk in our own life journey, it is much the same as we learn to hear His voice, step out, move forward, and sometimes actually catch the "perfect wave." His desire is to allow a spectacular ride – one where you wait, listen, and stand as you trust Him to take it from there. You ride with HIM as the wave moves up, slides forward, and beautifully delivers you down to the waiting sand. When you find that rhythm, you can't wait to slog back out, arduously paddle deeper, and push further into the deep. You know that as you wait patiently for this ride – this perfect wave of HIS plan, HIS direction, HIS purpose – patience will pay off and it will come. And when it comes – WOW! – it will be one spectacular ride.

Philippians 3: 13b-14 But one thing I do: forgetting what lies behind and straining forward to what lies ahead, I press on toward the goal for the prize of the upward call of God in Christ Jesus.

Personal Insights:

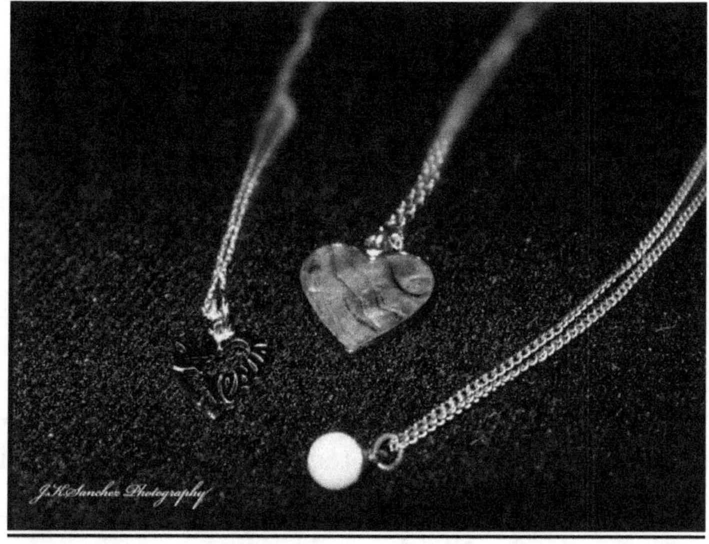

Tangled Chains

Today my jewelry box got some much-needed attention. With bracelets popping open the lid and necklaces spewing from the drawers, the answer was obvious: time-consuming sorting.

A bundle of tangled chains required the most attention; sitting for an extended time, picking patiently, unable to tug them apart for fear of breaking the delicate links. Oh, what a tangled mess.

The first one began to release – a heart with "Jesus" inscribed on it – and it quickly got my attention, as the Spirit began speaking. Then the second – a silver heart – unraveled in my hand.

Then one by one they simply untangled, ending with a silver pearl.

We are just like that mess of tangled chains!

Our lives are filled with tangled messes of both costume and precious jewels, all mixed together. As we live in that tangled environment, we are allowing our tangled thoughts and feelings and life's activities to ensnare us – causing the precious to become ineffective, and often forever lost.

When Jesus is our number-one focus, He begins the unraveling process. He gets our heart – and as we surrender to His untangling, the costume jewelry simply falls off and the pearl of great value remains.

As you contemplate your tangled life, consider giving all of your tangled chains into His hands and let the releasing begin.

John 10:27-28 My sheep hear my voice, and I know them, and they follow me. I give them eternal life, and they will never perish, and no one will snatch them out of my hand.

<u>Matthew 13:45-46</u> "Again, the kingdom of heaven is like a merchant in search of fine pearls, who, on finding one pearl of great value, went and sold all that he had and bought it.

<u>Personal Insights:</u>

In the Palm of His Hand

Last fall I planted a plethora of spring bulbs, hoping for a beautiful show when the frost, snow and bone-chilling cold had begun to recede. As the ground began to warm, those bulbs began to respond. And much to my delight, the bright-colored daffodils and tulips lifted my spirits as they bloomed.

It wasn't until the tulips burst into fullness that I was overwhelmed by a spiritual similarity. These tulips had been buried seven months; during the dark, wet, frozen winter they were not resting, but being prepared for one single purpose! All that waiting had allowed strength and nourishment to marinate within them. And at just the right time, they erupt and bring forth ONE single flower – one that had a purpose for just a few, precious weeks. That purpose, being to shout of His glory and the coming of spring, and with it, bringing extravagant hope!

The size of these tulips amazed me; they were so huge their bowl-base could fill the opened palm of my hand. And there you have it – in the palm of my hand.

We, too, are like that ONE single flower in the palm of our Father's hand. Our beauty and objective are single-focused for His purpose. We, too, go through times where we experience those months – or even years – of dark, wet, frozen winter. However, when we rest in the palm of His hand and allow His preparation, we will come forth to that one single purpose, too. That one single mission that we were designed for; to shout of His glory – to shout of the coming of spring – to bring hope to the hopeless!

So, if you are in that time where you feel buried – waiting in the dark, wet, frozen winter – take courage, for you are being prepared for that one single purpose! The ground will warm and thaw, and you will burst forth into your single mission for His glory.

Rest and allow His strength and nourishment to marinate within you; get comfortable in the palm of your Father's hand, for He has you and He is faithful to accomplish all that He has started.

Isaiah 49:16a Behold, I have engraved you on the palms of my hands.

Philippians 1:6 And I am sure of this, that he who began a good work in you will bring it to completion at the day of Jesus Christ.

Personal Insights:

____

____

____

____

____

____

____

Where Does My Help Come From?

"You are living in a 'rainbow and butterfly world' that is not reality." "How can you always be positive and only see beauty?" These are just a couple of the phrases that have been spoken at me during the last few years. But that is far from my living reality. I, too, live in a world full of struggles; physical, financial and emotional stressors tug daily; with whispering doubts and fears that could easily derail me. Every day I make a choice: my eyes look up – the only place that my strength can be found.

If you find yourself in one of the most difficult times of your life, whether it be physical injury or disease, emotional upheaval, relationship destruction or financial lack – there is only one place that your help can come from. You may be telling yourself that you don't care or that you don't have the strength or desire to even believe any more; however, Christ is standing there waiting, with open arms to hold you up and give peace where none can be found.

The enemy of our souls – the devil – comes to rob, kill and destroy all that surrounds us; he will raid all areas of your life. He steals your sleep, de-rails your thought processes, cripples your everyday movements and abilities, and dissolves your hopes and dreams. Days may come where you are too weak to get up from your bed, where you have barely slept due to pain, where there is no money for basic needs, or you stand holding a court-ordered ending of a relationship. But in the midst of any of these – YOU CAN look up!

Make a choice to look up – not down, inside, or even around you. Look to Christ – He has you, He carries you, He loves you, and is ALWAYS there for you. He is GOOD all the time – even in the darkest, most difficult places. During these times, you will find that His strength is your strength. When your strength is totally gone, He comes in and gives you hope, purpose and direction.

Through Christ, His strength floods in and you *can* be positive, you *can* see beauty and you *can* love living in a "rainbow and butterfly world." It is a specific decision to lift your eyes to the hills, and to be strengthened by His loving hand during your own weakness.

If you are living in the midst of pain and suffering, begin to look up for your hope – not down, in or around. Only when you lift your eyes to the face of Christ and allow Him into your pain and suffering, will you then be truly set free to live a life where that weakness will become your strength. You will step into a world where living a "rainbow and butterfly life" can be a reality.

2Corinthians 12:9-10 But he said to me, "My grace is sufficient for you, for my power is made perfect in weakness." Therefore, I will boast all the more gladly of my weaknesses, so that the power of Christ may rest upon me. For the sake of Christ, then, I am content with weaknesses, insults, hardships, persecutions, and calamities. For when I am weak, then I am strong.

Psalm 121:1-2 I lift up my eyes to the hills. From where does my help come? My help comes from the Lord, who made heaven and earth.

Personal Insights:

Thankful Simplicity

As a little girl, I was constantly skipping and singing. Wherever I went, I was skipping instead of walking – it was just more fun to get anywhere that way. I was always on the move.

I wasn't raised in a home where Jesus was priority; in fact, I thought bible stories were just stories, not real. We went to vacation bible school in the summer as an activity, and to church on Easter as a dress-up experience.

But somehow, when I was skipping all by myself, I would sing a little song of thanks. This little song was never the same because I saw something different every day. This little song wasn't even directed toward God, since I really didn't know him.

This little song was one of thankful simplicity. It went something like this: *thank you for my eyes, thank you for my feet, thank you for that bird, thank you for that bug...* As I skipped along, I simply called out simple thanks about all that surrounded me.

As I was reminded of this, my heart swelled; even then the love of Jesus was obvious to me – even when I didn't know Him. Today I find myself contemplating the importance of that thankful simplicity in our lives.

In a society of constant sound and busyness, we move through our lives without seeing the beauty around us; thankfulness is not part of our chaotic day. But to live and walk in the peace of Christ that is part of our inheritance, a thankful and rejoicing heart is a priority. Even during the hardest circumstances, we are promised that peace. It starts with a simple thankful response.

It's a choice! It's a decision! In the midst of tough times and in the center of your busy lifestyle, His peace is always available – it will still your anxious heart and settle your racing mind. But it all starts with refocusing your eyes – looking up and realizing the key is in simply being thankful.

Be childlike again – try moving (even skip, if you'd like) through your day with an attitude, or a song, of thankful simplicity.

Psalm 118:1 Oh give thanks to the Lord, for he is good; for his steadfast love endures forever!

Philippians 4:6-7 do not be anxious about anything, but in everything by prayer and supplication with thanksgiving let your requests be made known to God. And the peace of God, which surpasses all understanding, will guard your hearts and your minds in Christ Jesus.

Personal Insights:

____

____

____

____

____

____

____

____

An Audience of One

My love and passion for nature often leaves me mesmerized by the tiniest flowers that perch on top of weeds, intricately-lacy spider webs, the individual trill that each bird makes, and the multitude of other beauties I come across. So, it isn't new for me to be aware of the beauty I find in unexpected places. However, one morning I was stunned to find myself literally holding my breath in awe as I watched the most delicate ballet erupt over my flowers.

First, one gorgeous yellow-and-black butterfly moved in, hovering over the flowers. Then the dance began when a second and then a third joined in – not just random enjoyment of their floral feast –

but connecting one to another. Soon they swirled around like synchronized swimmers – looping, diving and softly fluttering. I could swear I heard music as I stood, totally amazed, and engrossed in what I was being allowed to witness.

I lost track of time as they continued, oblivious of my presence. The obvious joy that this dance provided to them was contagious to watch, and joy began to stir deep in my spirit as they presented this stunning ballet to their audience of one.

But soon, as if on cue, the dance was over; each butterfly flew off to different flowers, leaving me with a sense of profound amazement. I was humbly honored to have witnessed this intimate dance.

I began to contemplate what God's "deep meaning" must be for what I'd witnessed and experienced. Then, as if in answer to my question, laughter began to bubble up inside of me: there was no "deep meaning" – it was His simple gift of love, especially for me. WOW – now that truly was a "deep meaning!"

My day was filled with unimaginable joy because I took the time to stop what I thought needed to be done, and participated in what He allowed to float into my day.

My friend, don't miss one of God's unexpected interruptions by allowing your "to-do" list to distract you from the blessings He has planned for your day. Slow down and experience the gifts He has waiting all around you.

<u>*Psalm 84:1-4*</u> *How lovely is your dwelling place, O LORD of hosts! My soul longs, yes, faints for the courts of the LORD; my heart and flesh sing for joy to the living God. Even the sparrow finds a home, and the swallow a nest for herself, where she may lay her young, at your altars, O LORD of hosts, my King and my God. Blessed are those who dwell in your house, ever singing your praise!*

Personal Insights:

Shore Up Your Foundation

Foundations are built to support the style of home they are designed for. A single-family-dwelling foundation could never support an office building, just as, an office building foundation would be inappropriate for a single family. Foundations are in place to allow everyday living to prosperously move forward, and are also designed to withstand the environmental impact on the building that they support.

When storms, floods and earthquakes unexpectedly impact a community, often the homes still standing are those with strong foundations. The same applies to your spiritual life. Your spiritual foundation is built on Christ – the Word of God.

Your promise is a solid, unshakeable foundation that will weather any storm.

However, during your own impacting events – your personal storms, floods and earthquakes – you may often think that your foundation has been pulled out from under you and that it no longer exists. But once you have said YES to the Lord, He never walks away, never forgets you, and never pulls that foundation away – He knows your name.

2Timothy 2:19a But God's firm foundation stands, bearing this seal:
"The Lord knows those who are his,"

In the natural, we now have old, cracking, shifting foundations that can be lifted up, filled in and re-stabilized to return strength and support to a previously unusable building.

Though you have a promise spiritually, that says you never require that type of major repair; you can still find yourself needing some shoring up. It is an easy process: simply turn from where you find yourself and look up; the one who built your house stands there ready to complete all necessary repairs. He already paid for them – they belong to you, free of charge. He knows your name, the building He is building within you, and the purpose He desires to accomplish.

If you find yourself in a place where you perceive your foundation to be unstable in any way, don't hesitate, or continue living in that shaky building. Call your ultimate repair Man! The result is always a 5-star review – He only does perfect work.

Philippians 1:6 And I am sure of this, that he who began a good work in you will bring it to completion at the day of Jesus Christ.

Personal Insights:

____

____

____

____

____

____

____

____

Cloud by Day and Fire by Night

As Israel was led into the wilderness, the very presence of God was visually present to direct their way. By day a cloud guided them, and by night a fire gave them light; both leading them into the purposes of God, being a people who belonged to a living God.

The Holy Spirit presents as a type of internal '*cloud by day and fire by night.*'

As He is now dwelling within us, He is a gift given, a Helper introduced and a Comforter placed within. We find Him as that small, still whisper, a light leading us into the purposes of God – our true purpose is now being found as a child of the living God.

That voice, my internal *'cloud by day and fire by night'* has been present in my life for decades; bringing me comfort in the midst of loss, direction in the center of chaos, and peace and joy through this life's journey. His presence is a source of continual strength. He brings that whispered warning – that voice of instruction and encouragement – and His presence is what leads me daily into the purposes planned for my life before I was born.

As you hear a whisper beginning to stir, silently pulling your mind to its presence; the still, small voice of the Spirit of God is drawing your attention. He is present to bring you direction – both to lead and to warn – a constant presence of a loving God.

That voice, the voice within, the voice of the Holy Spirit, dwells in each of us and becomes louder as we listen. His presence can shape, correct and lead our lives as we step into a place of believing, receiving, and anticipating His whispered voice.

Today I walk as one who desires to follow that *'cloud by day and fire by night,'* – His presence now resides within me, His voice I lean into daily, His warnings I take seriously, His instructions I endeavor to follow spontaneously – living as one who belongs to my Savior, Jesus Christ, a true and living God.

Join me in this adventure – you will never be the same. Wait, listen and move as the Spirit directs – He will happily become your *'cloud by day and fire by night.'*

Exodus 13: 21-22 And the Lord went before them by day in a pillar of cloud to lead them along the way and by night in a pillar of fire to give them light that they might travel by day and by night. The pillar of cloud by day and the pillar of fire by night did not depart from before the people.

John 15:26 "But when the Helper comes, whom I will send to you from the Father, the Spirit of truth, who proceeds from the Father, he will bear witness about me."

Personal Insights:

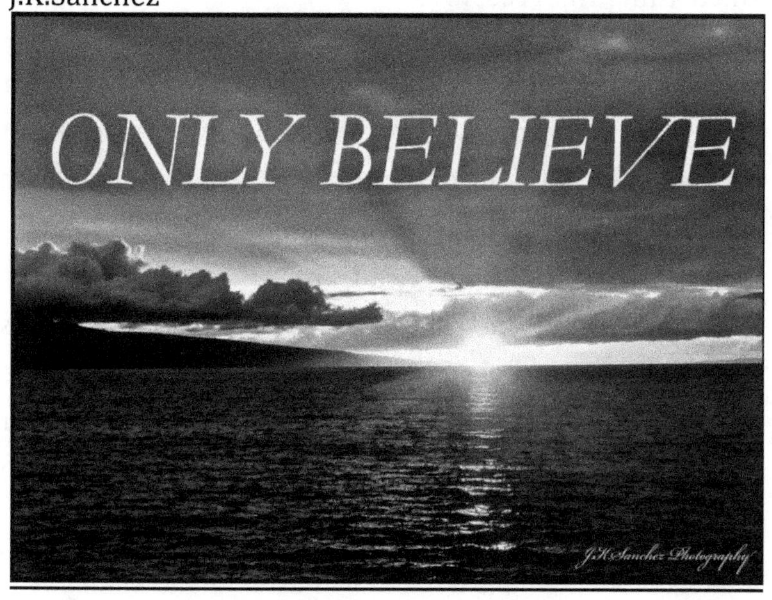

"But Why, Mommy?"

The question, "But why, Mommy?" erupts from little lips almost as soon as language skills appear; parents bombarded hundreds – if not thousands – of times as the child grows. Often the question, repeatedly asked will eventually evoke a firm response from us as parents: "Because I said so!" This answer to the child's mind is seemingly an appropriate answer; our little ones accept that we know the answer, that there is a reason, and that we have it under control. Acceptance and belief relieve the concern, and they run off to play.

As adults our need for answers continues. Our questions turn from, "But why mommy?" into, "But why God?" We still need answers, assurance and an understanding of, "everything is going to be OK."

We often cry and shout out those questions to God because of the hurts, disappointments and fears that riddle our lives. Our assurance and belief are missing, while anger and frustration become our seemingly-permanent state of being. Our need to understand and hear, "everything is going to be OK" wavers as we continue holding on to our rights and control. We find NO relief in our chaos. These needs outweigh the simple faith that we had as a child, though the answer is still the same: "Because I said so!" – which now is heard in our heavenly Father's voice.

There will still be the things that don't make sense: those that furrow your brow, cause your heart to pause and your head to shake. The difference is that, like a child, you can let it go because "Daddy said so." You can be assured of the answer and run off to play again.

Doubts and questions fill the bible – it's not something new to our time in history.

Believing has always been a choice that man has had to make. Jesus assured Jairus, even having just witnessed a miraculous healing, "Do not fear, only believe." We hear a father's response to the need for Jesus' deliverance for his son with quacking words, "I believe, help my unbelief." And then, of course, the story of Thomas who needed to see in order to believe. We have that choice to make also – deciding to lay down our *whys, hows* and *what ifs* as we choose to ONLY BELIEVE!

There are no platitudes or canned answers to help the tough, often horrific, life situations that we or our loved ones must suffer. But when you walk through these times, your only peace, comfort and strength will come from a solid belief: My God is a good God! He loves me, and I can accept His loving response of "Because I said so."

Return with simple, childlike faith and lay down the *why* questions; believe that Jesus loves you, that you are safe, and that He has it all under control.

Make that choice to ONLY BELIEVE!

John 20:27-29 Then he said to Thomas, "Put your finger here, and see my hands; and put out your hand and place it in my side. Do not disbelieve, but believe." Thomas answered him, "My Lord and my God!" Jesus said to him, "Have you believed because you have seen me? Blessed are those who have not seen and yet have believed."

Personal Insights:

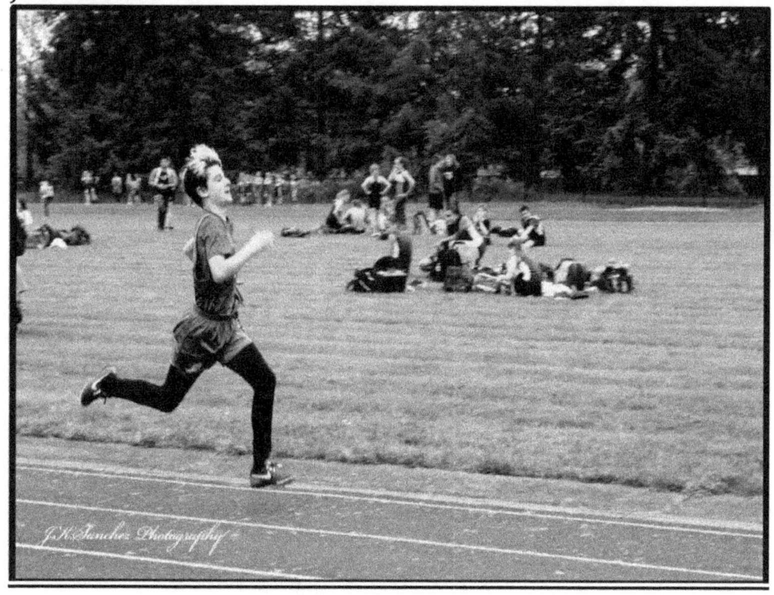

Run to Win

Recently I had the pleasure of cheering on the sidelines of a middle-school track meet. My favorite runner, my grandson, was barreling down the track, passing them all, and leaving most in the dust. This, the final meet of the short season, was a test to win: to beat all previously-run times – his own and all the other's. Oh, and run he did – with everything in him. With single focus, pointed directly toward that finish line, he pushed with every fiber, every cell and every breath to WIN! The sounds around him – the cheers of the crowd, the track at his feet, and even the pounding of his own heart – were not heard.

Every concern, discomfort, and thought were set aside for the joy of the run.

What we didn't see at this track meet was all the physical conditioning that was put in before today's "pop" of the starter's gun. That conditioning included daily pushing of those muscles that resulted in their throbbing pain at night, the pounding headaches from over exertion and rapid dehydration, and the skinned, torn, twisted tissue and tendons. These times – hidden from the cheering crowd – are the times where the decision to endure is won or lost.

We are on a similar track, a similar race: our life journey – our race. Our WIN is already promised – it belongs to us through the cross of Christ. But our race is not an easy one, it is meant to be RUN with endurance. It will require times of determination and physical conditioning. We must cross that finish line. We must have a single-focus on that prize! We must not hear nor allow all the distractions, concerns, and discomforts of daily life to overcome us. We must endure and push past the relational hurts and disappointments, financial struggles, physical illnesses and much more – all those throbbing, pounding, torn and twisted pieces that are part of this race of life.

Jesus already promised you the win – the decision is yours. IF you will endure to the finish line, IF you will focus on the prize – then this is the time where you decide to obtain it! Decide to run your race with endurance to receive the prize that is waiting at the finish line – and run it well – with every fiber, every cell, and every breath you have been given.

Run to Win – run for the joy of the run!

I Corinthians 9:24 Do you not know that in a race all the runners run, but only one receives the prize? So run that you may obtain it,

Hebrews 12:1 Therefore, since we are surrounded by so great a cloud of witnesses, let us also lay aside every weight, and sin which clings so closely, and let us run with endurance the race that is set before us,

Personal Insights:

God's "Today" Assignment

As the cool, early, fall morning covers my yard, I see activity in my filbert tree. Every year there comes a harvesting time for the local squirrels. We have grown to expect and joyfully watch when these few days arrive each year. It is fascinating to observe the acrobatics and diligent work that begins at sunrise, and continues to sunset, for several days in a row. Every nut is gathered, checked, shelled and tucked away for future use.

However, that tree has now grown to be nearing 20 feet tall, and this year I found myself holding my breath as my little woodland critters began this tenacious dance. They teeter on thin branches, pulling and shelling nuts. Then, as if the height doesn't matter; they jump and swing from branches high in the air to reach the next tiny treasure.

They have no fear, and nothing distracts them – even my yapping dachshunds, who circle the base of the tree. Their eyes are focused on the assignment at hand.

<u>*Proverbs. 4:25*</u> *Let your eyes look directly forward, and let your gaze be straight before you.*

We can learn a spiritual lesson from these little squirrels. They woke to have one assignment today, and that has been their job – and only job – all day long. Nothing distracted them from that purpose.

Jesus walked with so many needs and expectations circling Him every day, but He chose to focus on the voice of His Father, only doing what He was called to do. Thus, when His short three years of ministry was complete, He could say, "I glorified You on the earth, having accomplished the work which You have given me to do."

We allow everyday expectations and needs to pull us, run our lives, and distract us into exhaustion. We must choose to listen and obey the Spirit's voice. When we begin to say no and set down the managing of our own expectations – as well as others' expectations – we then begin to experience, with joy, the picking up of His specific assignments. We will be able to stay on task and have plenty of strength to accomplish what He desires for us to accomplish.

Just as my little squirrels focus only on the prize (the tiny nut treasure), our forward focus on God's assignment for TODAY will bring an eternal treasure and allow us to rejoice with the words that Jesus spoke, "I glorified You on the earth, having accomplished the work which You have given me to do."

Join me today in a choice to jump and swing from the highest branches, reaching for the next treasure: HIS assignment, set up just for you to complete. Willingly lay down those urgent things that distract, and open your eyes to His eternal plans for your TODAY.

Philippians 3:13-14 Brothers, I do not consider that I have made it my own. But one thing I do: forgetting what lies behind and straining forward to what lies ahead, I press on toward the goal for the prize of the upward call of God in Christ Jesus.

Personal Insights:

Sweet or Sour Grapes?

The sweet burst of flavor is anticipated as you hold a cluster of grapes in the palm of your hand. We have grown accustomed to enjoying this late-summer fruit, uninterrupted by the hard, woody appearance of the dreaded seed within our mouth. My preference is always *seedless* – how about you?

Spiritually, your fruitful growth comes by laying down your past at the feet of Jesus. You grow as you walk through trials with your eyes focused on His face. Faith then says to persevere – your persistence builds a trust that He has a specific plan for your life.

Ultimately, the growth of sweet, *seedless* grapes comes from a place where your faith – your trust in Jesus only – has been built over time.

Over the last decade, my husband and I have tried our hand at growing grapes. At one time we had seven vines containing five different varieties. All have grown prolifically, but we found that even those tagged as *seedless* still touted that woody seed. So several years ago, with chainsaw in hand, we took them to the ground.

Each year we have fought with those roots that have continued to shoot up. But this year, three finally conceded and died, and two produced only leaves – leaving us with just two to manage. But when our diligence lapsed, those two suddenly, had clusters growing. "Oh well," we decided, "Two won't be too bad to clean up after."

To our great surprise, they matured and the desire to "taste and see" outweighed the dreaded seed. The sweet burst of flavor was an unexpected experience, but the joy came when we found them *seedless.*

How did that happen?

As we learn to walk with our eyes focused on Jesus – not our circumstances or our past – amazing transformations occur in and around our lives.

Our internal and external environments shift, and to our great joy, our sour grapes become sweet and our woody seeds disappear. These changes come from persistence to sit in His presence, allowing His transformation to occur. He does all the cultivating, He feeds, sends the sun and the rain; we say "YES" and begin to receive and grow. Then suddenly, we taste the sweet burst of flavor – and with great joy, we find that we are *seedless* and full of His sweetness.

Join me by laying down your past and your current trials. Let's persistently pursue the presence of the Holy Spirit at the feet of Jesus. The transformation will be sweet!

II Corinthians 3:18 And we all, with unveiled face, beholding the glory of the Lord, are being transformed into the same image from one degree of glory to another.
For this comes from the Lord who is the Spirit.

Psalm 16:11 You make known to me the path of life; in your presence there if fullness of joy; at your right hand are pleasures forevermore.

Personal Insights:

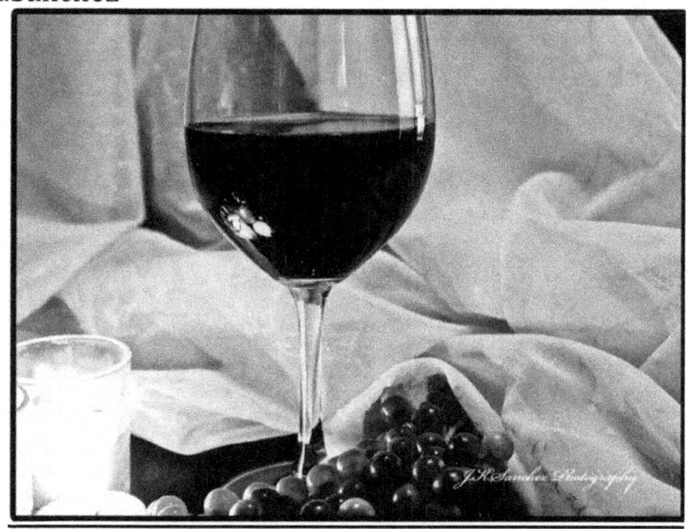

Ready to Stomp Grapes?

Making a good wine requires time, energy, and a lot of science. The process, from start to finish, can take years. The planting, tending and harvesting of the grapes is just the beginning; the chemistry kicks in later as the crushing, pressing and fermenting is launched.

Whenever we hear the word "crushing," it invokes a negative response. Anything that endures "crushing" will never be the same. But this process is necessary to make a good wine.

We have all laughed hilariously as we watched Lucy in the grape vat stomping the grapes, but that process is real. To get to the good stuff, the grapes must be crushed. The skins must be burst, the flesh must be mashed, and the stems dislodged. This whole process doesn't sound funny, but rather brutal. Once the crushing has occurred, there is a time of waiting that allows all those parts to mingle, creating a unique, complex flavor.

A number of years ago we endeavored to make our own wine. We learned what and when to do each step, as well as made many "oops-we-won't-do-that-next-time" mistakes. In our memories, one of the best parts was the crushing process. Though transforming our fruity jewels into a messy mush was physically difficult, the sweet aroma that enveloped us that day stirred anticipation of the ultimate outcome.

We often pray for *new wine* and ask for *new wineskins* from the Lord – but when the process begins, we pull away, run away, or cry out, "Why me, God?!" Understanding the process of making natural wine gives us a little insight into the spiritual process that "our Winemaker" undertakes in our lives in order to produce the very best wine from us.

Once the grapes are ripe – when all of our natural, spiritual maturing is complete – the process is just beginning. Our yielding to the process requires a deep trust. We must trust that He is in control of every aspect of our lives.

The crushing breaks the skin – the "me" – and allows the yeast of the Holy Spirit unrestricted access to the good stuff inside. The crushing breaks up the "all-about-me" thinking, changing us. We begin to look outside of ourselves to see a bigger picture than us alone. In the crushing process, all of the stems – the unimportant hooks of life – are pulled away. After a time of waiting that allows all those parts to mingle, a unique complex flavor will ultimately arise, moving us to the pressing phase.

What does the "crushing" look like and feel like? You may already find yourself there if you are in the middle of life's physical, emotional, mental or financial struggles. Not the everyday ones, but those that take everything out of you. Those times where you can only look up, focus on Jesus, and trust that He loves you and has the best for you. It's a time where you know you have nothing you can do yourself; it's here that you surrender, yielding to the "crushing" process.

There is nothing fun or funny when you find yourself in these difficult places of life. It is a brutal time. However, you are not alone – Jesus is there to pour out His love, encourage, and strengthen you.

So be courageous, look up, and fix your eyes on the one who loves you, and remember the outcome will be the very best wine possible as you choose to yield to the hand of your Winemaker.

<u>Romans 5:2-5</u> *Through him we have also obtained access by faith into this grace in which we stand, and we rejoice in hope of the glory of God. Not only that, but we rejoice in our sufferings, knowing that suffering produces endurance, and endurance produces character, and character produces hope, and hope does not put us to shame, because God's love has been poured into our hearts through the Holy Spirit who has been given to us.*

Personal Insights:

____

____

____

____

____

____

____

Into the Winepress

The scent of fermentation is distinctly nauseating. In wine making the fermenting process can't be rushed. Days pass as you find yourself periodically retching when a whiff catches you off guard. Finally, at just the right time, you can bring out the winepress. Its brutal archaic feel is needed to exert continuous force on this batch of crushed, fermented grapes. The pressing process now removes all the solid bits, and from it begins to flow pure, rich wine.

We don't think of the pressing process often; we take it for granted. We press many things without a second thought; juicing a lemon, rolling out cookie dough, ironing out wrinkles – all of which are a form of pressing. Applying pressure always changes the original form: a solid lemon becomes juice, a bowl-full of dough becomes a tasty, well-formed cookie, your just-out-of-the-dryer shirt changes from "a mess" into a smooth, presentable clothing item – all from that process.

When the Holy Spirit works the pressing process in your life, you must remember that His plan is always to change you – to transform you into *new wine.* He works on one batch at a time, and the process must be yielded to and walked through. How you choose to walk through it is the key: eyes on Jesus, trusting that He is in control, and laying down your "fix-it" mentality.

You have made it through the crushing and fermenting of this batch, but the pressing now begins. Yielding your heart, mind, body, and spirit to the loving hand of the Father will allow this process to bring forth a sweet wine.

The ultimate process of pressing results in leaving behind all that was "you" to become what you were planned for. The Holy Spirit's desire is to move you into a position of contact with the face of Jesus.

The pressing will release a free-flowing wine, and here you are changed. The pure, rich wine that flows, sends an aroma of worship to the Father that is intoxicating. It is a worship not made from man, not music or performance, but a purity of true worship that can only be found as you yield to the winepress.

II Corinthians 3:18 And we all, with unveiled face, beholding the glory of the Lord, are being transformed into the same image from one degree of glory to another. For this comes from the Lord who is the Spirit.

Personal Insights:

____

____

____

____

____

____

____

____

Does Your Barrel Leak?

The oak barrel sits, ready to receive its prize. No thought is given to what it has endured to get to this place. Once it was carefully constructed, the real preparation began; boiling, flushing, toasting, and more, befell this single barrel. The importance of each step will make the difference in its ability to keep the prize – one that is full of life, and is rich and desirable. The prize: new wine!

Spiritually, we talk of *new wine* with excitement and anticipation. We begin a frenzied chase to find it – conferences and concerts abound – but will you find it there?

You may experience a manifested encounter with the presence of God and be stirred for "more," but will it stay when you get home?

New wine poured into an unprepared vessel leaks out.

Just as the oak barrel is prepared for its prize, we, too, are prepared. However, it is not about "doing things" to get ready nor is it trying to pull it down from heaven – instead, it is about "being made" ready. Preparation for us looks similar to the barrel: we will go through the boiling, flushing, and toasting as we surrender to the loving hand of our heavenly Father.

As we hunger for the presence of God, that hunger stirs a deep love within, that love turns to desire, that desire erupts into a longing, and that longing pushes us to the feet of Jesus.

As we spend time in silent adoration at His feet, our heart solidifies with a mindset of yielding to only what is Him – something changes, and the vessel is prepared. As we choose to lay aside all the distractions, then we can choose to step into worship, into reading the word, into prayer, and into fasting – suddenly, we are there.

All of these choices are not about coercing God's hand, but about a love that is growing. This love desires His presence above everything else. This love to see His face and to hear His voice becomes a deep passion. In that place of passionate pursuit, we find His presence; there we begin to experience and hear Him – right there in our own living room His presence manifests. We become a vessel that He has prepared to carry and distribute His *new wine*. We no longer leak!

As we wait at His feet, He pours a continual flow of *new wine* in and through us. Then, as we walk into a gathering of passionate pursuers, we will enter an atmosphere that has been saturated in worship, word and prayer. The love, excitement and joy will pulse as a single heartbeat from the Father, and we will find ourselves in the presence of an explosion of Glory.

Every part of our lives will begin to have one central focus – Jesus! Our alignment to the Father's voice, His plans and purposes will stir a passion. This passion is to say "YES, LORD" as we live a lifestyle full of *new wine* from Heaven. We will see others drawn to us by the intoxication we are now walking under. They will ask, "Where have you been? Why does your face shine? How can I get what you have?" And sharing the gospel will be easy. Our prayers will change as we hear and do as the Holy Spirit directs. We will see His answers and miracles abounding all around us. Our faith will be WHO we are, not something we do.

Join me as we fight off the distractions, begin to walk a lifestyle of passion, and choose daily to sit at the feet of Jesus!

Be ready to say "YES, LORD" as He directs you to pour out *new wine* to those around you.

Matthew 9:17 Neither is new wine put into old wineskins. If it is, the skins burst and the wine is spilled and the skins are destroyed. But new wine is put into fresh wineskins, and so both are preserved.

Personal Insights:

____

____

____

____

____

____

____

____

____

The Bouquet that Surrounds Us!

Recently, while I was on a hunt for just the right flowers to add into a few new borders in my yard, the Holy Spirit began to highlight my love for flowers.

I love flowers – they just draw me in. From crocus and grape hyacinths that sprout through the frozen ground in early spring, to the huge, dinner-plate sized dahlias that stand in strength and presentation. From the beautifully-scented freesia, wisterias and jasmine, to ones with no scent, and even the adversely-scented flowers.

I am continually amazed at the beauty and diversity that God created in such a gorgeous bouquet, all just for us to enjoy.

BUT that's not all. What about the bouquet He has made out of all of us? Just as each flower is created completely different, so are we. Enjoying the differences in the flowers around us, is easy – but when it's differences in people, we tend to pull away from those who are different than us.

Instead of pulling away, separating and isolating into the "right" groups, He has created us to be a world-changing bouquet. Each of us with all our differing sizes, shapes and scents, complementing one another.

Take some time to look around and spend time with those who are different from you – and you will walk away smiling. You'll discover that people who are different are also pretty amazing. We were created to complement each other – to enjoy the differences of our brothers and sisters, and most of all, to love each other. Take time to enjoy the human bouquet that surrounds you.

I John 4:7 Beloved, let us love one another, for love is from God and whoever loves has been born of God and knows God.

Personal Insights:

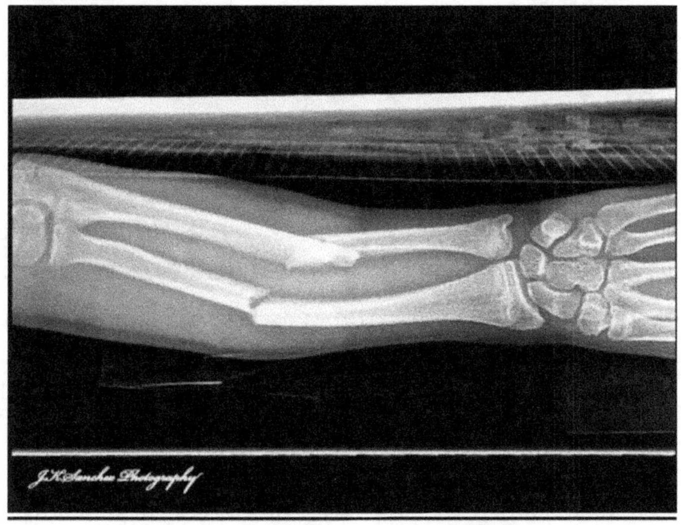

Broken Beyond Repair

Football practice wouldn't be the same today. With the snap of his arm bones, my grandson's hope for a winning season was broken before it began. Silence and chaos broke out all at once, quickly covering the field as realization of the accident spread. Amidst the shouting and ambulance siren, a calming voice from a trusted friend was heard, "It'll be alright. It's a clean break – it will heal."

Surgery would be required – not once, but twice – to repair this double-bone, compound fracture. But in the hands of a skilled orthopedic surgeon, it will heal and he will play again – life and his arm will be as good as new.

There are times in your life when you feel that you have been broken beyond repair. The tragic loss of a loved one looms over your heart. The betrayal of a trusted friend crushes your spirit. The angry, vicious words spoken against you grip your mind. But through the pain, there is a calming voice that can be heard, a whisper deep inside – He is speaking in the midst of that pain, "It'll be alright. You will heal – life will be good again."

Your brokenness can be healed – it's not quick, it's not painless, it's not easy – but the skilled hand of a surgeon can repair it. You have a skilled surgeon waiting for you – one who intimately knows the pain and hurt you are walking through.

Jesus is waiting; His surgery heals, restores, and gives new life. He is there, wiping every tear, whispering His love back into your broken heart, pouring restored trust into your broken spirit and eradicating lies from your mind. He's whispering, "Life will be good again."

When you feel you have been broken beyond repair, remember that in the hands of a skilled surgeon you will heal, you will play again, and life will be good. Trust your brokenness into the hands of Jesus – your Surgeon – He is waiting for you.

<u>Psalm 34:18</u> The Lord is near to the broken-hearted and saves the crushed in spirit.

<u>Psalm 147:3</u> He heals the broken-hearted and binds up their wounds.

<u>Personal Insights:</u>

Stuck in the Brush?

The darkness is filled with silence as the chill of the night causes him to pull a woolen blanket close around his shoulders. Tonight, his awareness of creatures quietly waiting and watching is heightened. The stones piled high make a quasi-safe barrier encircling his flock, but experience warns him that hidden danger waits all around – hungering to make a meal of his little ones.

The open entrance gives access not only to those who are permitted, but also to those who would steal and kill; so here is where he sits on this dark night, here is where he will lay down across this entrance to rest as the night wears on.

His mind wanders to the afternoon's activities. As he had begun taking stalk of his sheep, readying for his evening gathering, one was missing.

He thought of nothing but that one lost sheep. He searched through the brush, down the mountain side, by the river, and anywhere this little one might have gone. He never once thought of the ninety-nine others that he had left behind as he searched for his lost one. He knows each sheep personally – its looks, characteristics, habits and movements. To this shepherd, each sheep is as individual as a human. Each one holds a special place in his heart. This has happened many times to him, and each time the love he has for that lost one, overwhelms him as he persistently traverses dangerous terrain – never thinking of himself – only thinking of that one.

Thankfully, today, the lost one was found. It had wandered off all alone and soon had become tangled under brush, unable to free itself. The shepherd called it by name and, with loving hands, reached down and set it free. He lifted this tired little one out of the entrapment, drew the quivering body close, and with joy, placed it over his shoulders to carry it back to a place of safety within the flock.

Just like that little sheep, we can find ourselves tangled under many different entrapments, unable to free ourselves. We wander off, away from the safety of the flock, or – even worse – are snatched from the flock by claws and jaws desiring to steal and kill us. But look up! For you have a good, good Shepherd who knows you by name. With great love and without hesitation, He will leave all the rest, just for you.

He desires to free you! You can never get so far away from Him that His great love will not find you. You can never hide from Him where His love and persistence won't search for you. Your anger at Him cannot separate you from the love He has for you.

If you find yourself stuck in a lost, empty place, simply listen and look up! You will find Him calling your name, and He will be right there to free you and draw you close. With great joy, He will place you over His shoulders and triumphantly carry you to safety.

Luke 15:4-6 *"What man of you, having a hundred sheep, if he has lost one of them, does not leave the ninety-nine in the open country, and go after the one that is lost, until he finds it? And when he has found it, he lays it on his shoulders, rejoicing. And when he comes home, he calls together his friends and his neighbors, saying to them, 'Rejoice with me, for I have found my sheep that was last.'*

Personal Insights:

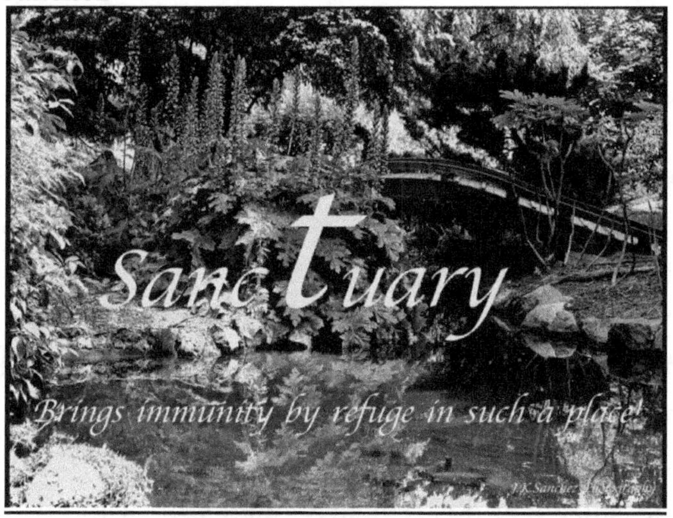

Sanctuary
Brings immunity by refuge in such a place!

A Sanctuary Within

Today, I look out into my personal outdoor retreat and see a plethora of birds of all species, as well as my hummingbird friends who fill the skies throughout the day. Then, joining them, butterflies swoop in and out to nibble on my flowers. What began eighteen years ago has become an amazing sanctuary for birds and butterflies – and *me!* The peace of God surrounds every area we have lovingly created.

Any morning I can walk through my yard and find birds and butterflies abounding, and an unexpected peace settles over me. As I contemplate those mornings, the word "sanctuary" stirs in my heart.

Thankfulness grows within, as I look at my little paradise: a not-so-big home and one way-too-big yard that has matured over our eighteen years of caregiving.

Our yard, with its enormity, overwhelmed us many times over these years. But my vision of what it was meant to be has slowly evolved. Now, after many hours and years filled with work, the vision has slowly come to pass as our little park has materialized, and is regularly filled with wildlife.

Also, my little home has often been filled to the bursting point at family gatherings. My family has grown – by births and marriages, as well as by those who have been added for simply no other reason than our love for each other.

Additionally, there have been the times when we have opened our home to those in need of a place of refuge. We have often questioned, "Why us?" But we have also matured, just as the house and yard have, and now realize it was His love that has drawn them to our home – our sanctuary. We have simply said "yes" to His request, and invited them in. In some small way, we have been allowed to help them heal. The broken, the needy, and those needing a little "TLC" have been restored and released to the next steps in the journey that God had begun for them.

Paralleling this long-term creation in the natural to our spiritual walk, I realized that TIME is required to truly see and experience the sanctuary that God has created within us and around our lives. As we continually turn construction over to Him, He digs, plants and moves things in and out – and suddenly His peace is reigning – we begin to SEE the fruit and are blessed to enjoy it. It is always after much has been done – hard work and the mess cleaned up – that the beauty presents itself and fruit is flourishing.

As we allow the loving hand of Christ to create His sanctuary within us, we are allowed the great joy of being a part of the same process of creation in others. In love, we pour out His healing and His restoration, and encourage the release of His children into who He created them to be.

Our lives then become a place filled with love, peace and refuge, which draws others in to this "God place" of sanctuary.

Willingly step into the process. Allow His hand and TIME to pour over and through you, as the sanctuary within you develops and grows, and is allowed to pour over those around you.

Isaiah 32:17-18 And the effect of righteousness will be peace, and the result of righteousness, quietness and trust forever. My people will abide in a peaceful habitation, in secure dwellings, and in quiet resting places.

Personal Insights:

Extravagant Shopping - Just Ask

I am not a shopper – sorry ladies, I just am not. I have my list, go in, get it, and out the door; I am a single-focused shopper. But, there is one place that overwhelms me – where the dormant "shopper gene" erupts: a nearby heavenly plant nursery. When I arrive there and walk into this amazing paradise, every sense and desire begins stirring, bringing euphoric joy within me.

Over the years I have been lovingly forbidden to enter this paradise unless finances are lucrative, since I never leave without shopping well. I have learned to wait, watch and ask for my desires – then my “extravagant shopping" happens.

I know you are asking, what does shopping have to do with anything spiritual?

Just like when my eventual "extravagant shopping" is set in motion, our prayers are extravagantly provided for because HE is able. We ask, He hears and at His perfect time our shopping needs arrive.

HE WHO IS ABLE is my provider. HE does *far more, abundantly beyond all that I ask or think* – and that's WAY more than I can ever ask for.

Often, we think that what we desire or need is just too small to ask God for, or that we don't matter enough or that He won't answer it. But that's not who HE is – HE IS ABLE and HE loves you.

HE wants to extravagantly pour out over your life! Just ask!

Ephesians 3:20 Now to him who is able to do far more abundantly beyond all that we ask or think, according to the power at work within us.

I John 5:14 And this is the confidence that we have toward him, that if we ***ask*** *anything according to his will he hears us.*

Personal Insights:

Face-to-Face, Heart-to-Heart

I go to sleep and wake up to a handsome face that has been next to me for over forty years. I know his eyes, his mouth, his smile, his hands, his voice, and even his growing wrinkles; the interesting part is that this man looks the same to me now as he did in his 20's. I know him face-to-face; heart-to-heart; for we have become one.

Jesus knows us the same. He calls us to that type of relationship and communication.

He knows every hair, every wrinkle, and even every thought. He knows us intimately and asks us – desires for us – to come close and know Him face-to-face, heart-to-heart.

Intimacy comes from knowing, and knowing takes time – time at His feet, time in quiet stillness. A face-to-face, heart-to-heart connection. A hurried, "Hello, have a great day," or a quick on-your-way-out-the-door kiss will not work. No relationship is built on fast-paced connection, it is all about spending time.

This type of face-to-face, heart-to-heart adoration changes you at your very core. All the worries of the day, fears of the night and life's craziness falls away, and peace rushes in.

As my husband's presence brings me overwhelming love and joy, just because he is who he is, so does a face-to-face, heart-to-heart walk with Jesus bring an abundant life filled with joy – deep down joy.

What does it take? How do you get there?

Desire it! Ask for it!

Take TIME! SLOW down!

Wait silently! Sit and LISTEN!

And extravagantly ENJOY it!

The best part of your day will be waking up to HIM; for you will walk face-to-face, heart-to-heart, with your Savior.

Psalm 46:10 "Be still, and know that I am God"

Personal Insights:

____

____

____

____

____

____

Are You Prepared for Battle?

Digging in a field for water, several men unearthed a burial ground filled with treasures of ancient history. Artifacts dating deep into history were found, not only giving us a glimpse of the past, but also as an interesting spiritual abstract.

Amongst the Terra-cotta statues of warriors and horses, they found empty helmets and armor. Intricately designed, yet left empty – these pieces were made from limestone, each with hundreds of carved pieces mounted together. They had never been worn, but placed as a remembrance to the fallen. If these tributes had been worn, they would not have held up to a battle – they would have shattered on impact. The standard helmet and armor where designed from leather. Each piece was cut and lacquered, layered and mounted together, individually made to cover and withstand the weapons of the time.

The inference is that those who had fallen were not adequately prepared for the battle.

We, too, must prepare for battle!

How does that happen?

We prepare our helmets by making choices. First to believe in Christ's blood and its redemptive power. Our preparation is begun by studying the Bible and in living a lifestyle of love and prayer. Spending time diligently carving those pieces of leather as we consistently cover them with lacquer (the blood of Christ), which gives strength to them. Then we begin layering and mounting them together as we walk in faith as a follower of Christ.

We also must allow the carving, lacquering and mounting of life's journey, these become the pieces of our armor. They are fashioned by the Spirit of God. The process develops through His presence in our lives. He becomes our strength as faith surges and drives us to fight forward through the hardest, darkest places that we encounter as life's journey marches forward.

Often, life does not look or feel fair as its twists and curves are thrown at us, but each of those twists and curves (if allowed) will become a piece of armor being layered and mounted – strengthening our faith.

My desire is to be found wearing a strong, intact helmet and armor that has been designed by my Father's hand, covered with the blood of Christ, and strengthened by a walk of faith – and NOT to be found wearing one made of limestone – that is empty or shattered.

Fight forward, my friend! Choose today how you want to march into battle.

Ephesians 6:10-11 Finally, be strong in the Lord and in the strength of his might. Put on the whole armor of God, that you may be able to stand against
the schemes of the devil.

Personal Insights:

Two Faithful Caterpillars

I recently dreamt of two beautiful, fuzzy caterpillars. I watched them faithfully plod along the path set before them. They traversed the thick, wet grass and the stony, hot ground; they climbed straight up the slippery leaves, and triumphantly crawled over barriers of debris. Always moving up and over the most difficult of terrain and always moving forward, side-by-side, without hesitation on this journey of life. When cocooning began, together they allowed this process to begin as they hung side-by-side.

Then, as the sun rose on one morning, they awoke to a "suddenly" (an unexpected change) in their short lives.

On this day, there would be no pushing forward; the journey had changed. The sun's warmth, shining upon them, stirred something within as they slowly rose on the gentle breathe of a breeze. Together, they looked below at the path they had traveled; that journey, now looked so different from above. That "yesterday life" had been so full of wonder as they had fully lived each day – but in an instant, it was new. They now had been transformed from a caterpillar into a butterfly. A transformation that now allowed them to rise high above; to walk into a new eternal home where the caterpillar journey of short duration would now be used for an eternal purpose as a butterfly.

We, too, will someday be transformed from this life into a more glorious, eternal one. We know not when or how that will come to pass, but in faith we walk out our journey – plodding along the path set before us each day, traversing the thick, hot, slippery terrain we call life. We live each new day to the fullest, slowly and faithfully moving toward the ultimate prize: our own "suddenly." In that one moment, the Son will warm us and we will rise on the breeze to look below at what no longer matters.

In that instant, our eternal journey will have begun.

Philippians 3:20-21 But our citizenship is in heaven, and from it we await a Savior, the Lord Jesus Christ, who will transform our lowly body to be like his glorious body by the power that enables him even to subject all things to himself.

Personal Insights:

____

____

____

____

____

____

____

____

About the Author

J. K. Sanchez – Author, Graphic Design and Publisher

J.K. grew up in Las Vegas - fleeing the heat - she and her husband escaped to the Pacific Northwest 3+ decades ago. Her savored moments are those spent with her husband – the love of her life, as well as her children and grandchildren. Two dachshunds at her feet keep her days active as she spends her retired time saturated in her passions for photography, growing flowers and of course writing.

As an author and photographer J.K.'s love for people and nature is portrayed both through visually descriptive prose (devotional-studies in Nature vs Spiritual, non-fiction short stories and essays) as well as through the eye of the camera. Her spiritual passion for worship and the presence of the Lord draws her continually to see freedom proclaimed and released to others through the finished work on the cross of Jesus.

As an author, her books include: a 4 book devotional series (Winters Rest (2014), Spring's Assurance (2015), Summer's Delight (2015), Fall's Yield (2015)) Inspirational collection (Reflection of His Glory (2015)), Multiple journals and a Prayer Journal (Access to the Throne (2017)) and an inspirational collection of true stories written with 20 additional authors (Oh My God You Are Really Real (2018)) as well as contributor to (Keeper of the Faith (2016) and contributing author in Guideposts Angels on Earth Mar/April 2019)

As a photographer she has participated throughout Washington in gallery events and fairs, has photographed weddings, memorials, children, pets and personal portraits, currently has a published CD of her graphic landscape photographs (Names of God (2016)) as well as contribution of photographs for (Keeper of the Faith (2016)).

Her books are available on amazon.com as well as J.K.Sanchez.com

She is also available at
facebook.com/authorJKSanchez
facebook.com/majesticreflections
facebook.com/JudyKSanchezPhotography
And don't miss her current blog at
unearthinghistreasures.wordpress.com
Email: jksanchez.author@gmail.com

Titles available by J.K. Sanchez

Majestic Reflection Devotional Study Series:

Winters Rest

Spring's Assurance

Summer's Delight

Fall's Yield

Stand alone or companion journals:

Winters Rest Journal

Spring's Assurance Journal

Summer's Delight Journal

Fall's Yield Journal

Majestic Reflection Journal

Reflections of His Glory Journal

Oh My God You Are Really Real Journal

Additional Titles

Reflections of His Glory

Access To The Throne! – A Prayer Journal

Oh My God You Are Really Real

Contact me at: JKSanchez.author@gmail.com

Jksanchez.com Also find me on Amazon.com

www.ingramcontent.com/pod-product-compliance
Lightning Source LLC
LaVergne TN
LVHW051236080426
835513LV00016B/1619